Joy
in the
Morning

JOY IN THE MORNING
A Book to help the Bereaved

Copyright © 2008 by Vera Smith

Information address:
SPRINGS CHRISTIAN LITERATURE
63a Kilvergan Road, Lurgan, Co Armagh
N. Ireland, BT66 6LJ

First Edition
ISBN 978-0-9549225-2-8

Produced by:
TH JORDAN LTD
1a Millar Street
Belfast BT6 8JZ
N. IRELAND
028 9045 0866

www.thjordanltd.com

*"Weeping may endure for a night,
but joy comes in the morning."*

Psalm 30:2

Table of Contents

Foreword

Preface

Acknowledgements

PART TWO

Foreword

My kind friend, Miss Vera Smith, has given me the honour of writing the foreword for **Joy in the Morning**. I have known Vera for over twenty years, and for a time she worked with me as a colleague in that large and busy congregation of First Portadown Presbyterian Church.

Through sharing in ministry to many people who had lost a dear one, Vera saw the sorrow and loneliness which follows bereavement. She sought to carry the burden and feel the pain of such friends in a very real way, spending many hours sitting where they sat, often going far beyond the call of duty to do so.

This insightful book is her Biblical reflection on those experiences, designed as helpful thoughts for those labouring along that lonesome valley of losing someone special.

Death is something of which we all may be certain. Sooner or later it comes to each of our homes and hearts. It is always a shock - painful, difficult, sending our emotions into a spin and altering our routines and responsibilities. That is especially true if that loved one was particularly close to us. Bereavement can be a shattering experience, requiring a lengthy period to re-adjust to our new circumstances.

For those who are Christians we must remember "Jesus wept" when his friend Lazarus died. He can and does identify with us in our sorrow, and for every child of God, because Jesus died and rose again, there is HOPE.

"Christ in you, the hope of Glory."

My prayer is that **Joy in the Morning** will help to lighten the darkness and ease the pain of every soul struggling to cope with the loss of someone precious to them.

DESMOND KNOWLES

Preface

Navigating your way through grief is one of the most difficult journeys you will ever make. It is painful because it involves the deepest emotions.

I have spent the last anxious hours with individuals and families as together we have watched the loved one face the last great enemy, death, and go out into eternity. I have felt utterly helpless to ease their pain, although many have come back to express their appreciation of the help given.

No words of mine can prolong life! No gesture can console a breaking heart! The call has come and the 'carers' express their helplessness with understanding glances at family members. In the numbness of those parting moments, the world stands still. With hearts pounding, the sorrowing loved ones turn their tear-stained faces and embrace each other without uttering a word. Words sound clumsy: besides, nothing can convey the depth of feeling and emotion!

Silence seems to communicate the grief, as one by one the family move to a hospital corridor or a waiting room to talk together. Then, as if wakening from a bad dream, the question comes –What next?

When someone has said to me, "Vera, I cannot face another day!" I have wanted to prolong my visit to help further, but the telephone rings, someone knocks on the door and I have left a breaking heart, knowing they have to bravely face another kind friend, who wants to offer sympathy.

As a result of my experience in counselling the bereaved, I have felt the need to write this book. Often I would browse through the shelves in bookshops, read new publication materials, and, although there is some excellent material available on bereavement, I felt unable to find a book I could give to someone facing the first traumatic days and weeks of their bereavement, when the wound is so raw.

I left a broken hearted woman whose husband had died suddenly, she was unprepared for the trauma, lamenting,

"I didn't even get saying 'Goodbye' to him!"

I searched the bookshops and my library, but failed to be able to find a book suitable for someone whose concentration is limited because of pain. When a shop assistant said to me, "That's all we have!" I felt I did not have the right tool for the work I was doing. I do not have all the answers, but I trust you will find help as you read …

'Joy in the Morning'.

Acknowledgements

Joy in the Morning could not have been written without the help of a lot of people. I acknowledge the encouragement, prayers and support of a number of close friends, who inspired me and shared the vision of a book to help the bereaved. When the task seemed insurmountable, they listened, spoke words of wisdom, and encouraged me when I felt I would not achieve my goal.

How could I adequately express my thanks to those who have given me time and shared their experience in the hope that someone will find help in similar circumstances? I have deeply appreciated their openness and willingness to allow me to enter their hidden world of grief and then to share some of the pain, of their particular bereavement, through Joy in the Morning.

Thanks to Rev Desmond Knowles, who wrote the Foreword for the book, having meticulously read the manuscript. I am grateful to him for the love and pastoral care I observed in over twenty years, and especially when I was the recipient of his help in bereavement: to him and his wife Laura, for their example in identifying with the pain of losing a loved one, and in post bereavement care.

Special thanks to Bill Burnett, my main proof reader. He was helpful when I was working to dead lines and patient when I needed to 'pick his brain'. Also to Eleanor Watkins for proof reading the script and for her comments. George Russell, Dennis Flannigan and Bill Burnett were my very helpful advisory committee and their input was invaluable – My special thanks to them and to their wives who were the excellent back-up team!

My thanks to Ian, Gail and baby William for the front cover photograph which has special significance. Baby William was born after his grandfather died and will have "Joy in the Morning", when he meets his Granddad for the first time! Thanks also to photographer, Justin O'Neill, for permission to use the photograph for the front cover, and the photo of his daughter.

Information can be found on the Justin O'Neill website: www.justinoneillphotography.co.uk

I acknowledge the help of Billy Austin for advice in graphics, Barbara Hunter for her sketches and those who gave permission to use photographs.

Thanks to my family for their support and loving care during the writing of the book and for all their encouragement; thanks to IT student, Paul Smith, for his time and expertise in getting my PC up and running when I had problems.

Where possible I have sought permission for copyright to use quotes, poems etc., if this has been omitted, it has not been done intentionally.

TH Jordan and their staff could not have been more helpful. To Jim, John, Sharon and the team, I am most grateful. There are others, whose help has been invaluable in what has proved a special task.

Above all, my gratitude is to the "God of all comfort", for guiding me in ways that were outside of my control. My meeting with the right people, at the right time, was something that time and time again, amazed me: the sense of His presence as I wrote – I was aware that many people were praying for me and for that I want to personally express my sincere thanks.

DAY 1

LOSING SOMEONE SPECIAL

READING: John 11: 20 - 27

"Lord, if You had been here, my brother would not have died."

JOHN 11:21

As the sun rises in the east and a new day dawns, you waken to the realisation that you have lost someone very special. You never imagined a day when you would have to face the parting. You feel numb! You are confused as you struggle with disbelief. Suddenly, your world has changed - you have been plunged into sorrow and you feel unable to cope.

Your mind fills with unanswered questions, but you must go on! You know you must meet people: you seek courage, but it is elusive: you breathe a little prayer for help, but God seems far away.

Already, you have come through a stressful time watching and waiting; trusting that every moment, there would be a change and your dear one would bounce back to be spared a little longer with you. Mentally and physically exhausted, you breath a little prayer for help.

As friends comfort you and the shock and feeling of numbness, comes like waves, you are left shattered. Like so many others who have suffered loss, you thought it would never happen to you. It was always happening to someone else! Now the voice of your loved one is silent and your heart aches. The moment has come when you are alone with your thoughts. Questions keep coming but no answers. Hope is elusive.

When death enters our home, it brings sadness. Friends comfort us and we deeply appreciate their kindness and concern for us, but the moment comes when we are alone with our thoughts and nobody seems to be able to help – not even your dearest friend. It is then that God steps in to help, and whispers,

> "My grace is sufficient for you for My strength is made perfect in weakness."
> **2 CORINTHIANS 12:9**

At this moment your heart cries within you – there is numbness, disbelief and pain; for some it can be a physical pain. You may even feel you are having a heart attack. To attempt to describe it would be impossible for it is so deep nothing can reach it: or nobody can enter your private world of inner pain. You feel alone! You doubt that God understands your loss. He does understand for He suffered too. He watched His only Son hanging on the cross when He took the punishment for the sin of the world. God the Father, could not look on His beloved Son becoming our substitute and taking our rightful punishment, by dying "the just for the unjust that He might bring us to God!"

Jesus understands your pain, more than you even realise. When Martha met Jesus, she was suffering from shock, thus her exclamation – or perhaps accusation.

"Lord, if you had been here, my brother would not have died."
John: 11:21

Martha was giving vent to her pent up feelings, and the pain of losing her dear brother, whom she and her sister Mary loved. She was asking 'why?', and could find no answers. In her pain she felt if only Jesus had been there, He could have done something. He could have saved them this heartache. You may have said, 'If…' in your present loss too, but there does not seem to be an explanation.

Be assured that God is at your side, the Saviour, who was, "a man of sorrows" (Isaiah: 53: 3), is praying for you, and the Holy Spirit is present to strengthen you. Although Martha was unaware of it, Jesus knew all about her situation. He knew that both she and her sister Mary needed help, and He came at the right time.

He comes to you today to assure you that He knows about your grief and asks you to trust Him. He will not fail you!

Your friends are praying for strength for you to cope today, tomorrow, the next day and in the future.

New Hope

When battered by the storms of life,
can God help me cope?
When I sit back and question Him –
can He bring me new hope?
Oh, yes He can! Oh yes He can!
There's comfort in your grief -
for He who wept when Lazarus died
is near to bring relief!

DAY 2

THE VALLEY OF THE SHADOW

READING: Psalm 23

"Yea, though I walk through the valley of the shadow of death,

"I will fear no evil;

"For You are with me;

"Your rod and Your staff, they comfort me."

PSALM 23: 4

When a loved one passes through the Valley of the Shadow of Death, a door closes and another one opens. For the departed one, who dies trusting in Jesus Christ, it is the gateway to eternal bliss, for to be "with Christ is far better." Philippians: 1: 23.

For those who grieve, they turn to face a different valley. It is a valley of grief. Many questions flood the mind and there seems to be no answer. Where do I go from here? Where can I go for help? Will I ever be the same? No answers seem to come to meet the deep ache in your heart: inside there is a wound festering that you feel will never heal. Your happy world of love and friendship has reached an abrupt end.

As you enter your valley of mourning, it will take time for the facts to become clear. Let others help carry your load as they offer practical support in your time of need. They are available for you and want to feel needed, so just let them talk to friends, make the cups of tea and generally use their gift to be your friend.

Those closest to you will watch and when they see you need them they will be there for you when you want to talk and will understand when you have had enough. Trusted friends will help you work your way through the first traumatic days of your bereavement.

Because you have been stretched emotionally with the trauma, you may feel closer to your friends than you do to your heavenly Father, but you know you need a higher power to take you into the future. So many people are around you who want to comfort you, but know you need time to be alone, in order to come to terms with what has happened.

When you need to steal away from people, they will understand and wait for the appropriate time to talk to you. There is a time to be alone, so let others talk to your friends who have called to bring you sympathy. They will want to speak to you personally and assure you of their sympathy, but don't feel you have to talk for long, as you will be exhausted. It is in the quietness you will discover God's comfort and strength.

The God, who assured King David in Psalm 23, comes to you and wants to speak into the depths of your sorrow. Let Him be your Shepherd.

It will not be easy but with the Good Shepherd going before you, you can make it. Put your hand into the hand of the Shepherd and trust Him to lead you beside still waters. There you will feel the quietness of God's Holy Spirit strengthening you for the uphill climb facing you today and all your tomorrows. Keep reminding yourself of His promises. He will not fail you in your hour of need!

At this stage, you do not see a purpose, but let your mind dwell on the fact that for your loved one, who died trusting in Jesus Christ, "…to die is gain." Philippians 1:21.

Death is Gain

When I reach the boundary and step out of time,
  the Saviour will be there – say, 'child you are mine'!
I'll go with Him gladly, for He knows what's best
  He'll take my weak spirit to realms of the blest.

When I reach the Jordan, I know He'll be there
  to take me to mansions He went to prepare:
Death's valley He'll brighten for He is the Light;
  no darkness will linger – It's only 'goodnight'!

When I reach the Glory, how glad I shall be
  to waken in heaven and my Saviour see:
the mysteries now hidden, will all be made plain –
  as fulfilled are the scriptures –"to die is gain!"

DAY 3

THE WAITING SAVIOUR

READING: John: 20: 14 – 18

"She turned herself back, and saw
Jesus standing, and did not know it
was Jesus".

JOHN: 20: 14

Often in our grief, we become introvert and fail to recognise
the Saviour.

The story of Mary Magdalene is one of tenderness and
understanding. Mary is one of those who watched the
agonizing death of the Lord Jesus and performed an
honourable act by anointing His body for burial. The risen
Christ honoured her by allowing her to be the first to see Him
after His resurrection. When she saw Him she did not know
Him, though her heart was crying with intense yearning. As
she stood talking to the angel, there was someone behind her,
and she turned - It was Jesus! She did not recognise Him.
Was she too preoccupied with her sorrow that she failed to
recognise the One who could help her? Certainly, He was the
One she least expected to meet. It was her grief, that brought
her to the garden in the hope that she might find some
consolation; yet she failed to recognise Him.

It could be today, you too realise that Jesus has been standing at your side to comfort you and because of your deep grief; you have failed to recognise Him. Probably one of the reasons Mary did not recognise Him was because her eyes were filled with tears. Perhaps you are the same and through your tears, you have not recognised the One who is your best Friend and who wants to comfort you. He whispers 'fear not' and reminds you that your loved one is with Him in Paradise.

Jesus said to the dying thief who repented in the last moments of his life – "Assuredly, I say to you, today you will be with Me in Paradise." Luke 23:43

A painter took his canvas and painted a mother in deep distress; close to her was an angel bending over her to comfort her, his fingers touching at the same time the strings of the harp in his hands. He skilfully painted the young mother who was so absorbed in her own grief that she neither saw nor heard the angel and his celestial music. Her heart goes uncomforted and still breaking while the comfort is nearby. Is the Saviour trying to comfort you today? Please let Him!

Do Not Fear

He comes to heal the broken heart,
to wipe the falling tear:
to say 'fear not, I'll give you strength,
just lend a listening ear!'
His gentle voice comes soft and clear,
He whispers, 'Do not fear'
just place your hand in mine, my child
I see your falling tear!

DAY 4

COMFORT IN SORROW

READING: Isaiah 61: 1 & 2

"He has sent me… to comfort all who mourn."

ISAIAH 61:1

Isaiah foretold the advent of a Saviour and, in the fullness of time, the prophecy was fulfilled. Jesus came humbly to a Bethlehem stable – was born of the Virgin Mary and lived a sinless life, died an atoning death and now lives to make intercession for us.

You wonder how you could ever be happy again. Let Him minister to you today. He is the only One who understands your grief. He wants you to trust even though you do not understand. He wants to bring the rays of His sunshine into your life and help you to face the future.

Those who have had bereavement have testified to the faithfulness of a loving heavenly Father who has ministered to them and given special grace in their time of need.

Perhaps you say, "You don't understand!" I know I can never understand the depths of your grief. Nobody ever understands the pain of another in bereavement - each of us will deal with grief differently.

I have lost family members and I have sought to bring comfort to others passing through the 'Valley of Sorrow'. In each situation in helping others, I have to confess, I may not have made the right approach or helped in the situation, but have always committed the dear one to God praying that He would minister in His own unique way.

Our greatest comfort is the Word of God! The fact that Jesus said, "I am the resurrection and the life; he who believes in Me, though he may die, he shall live", is the greatest source of comfort, I can find. Your loved one, who died resting in Jesus Christ as Saviour and Lord, is alive and the great hope for the Christian is – we shall meet again!

No Answers

Though I don't understand
the mystery of pain –
I know that in nature
it takes sunshine and rain
for the earth to produce
an abundance of grain.

Though I don't understand
the mystery of pain –
I know God understands
and will one day explain
that the dark threads of life
were for spiritual gain.

DAY 5

A LOAD TOO HEAVY TO CARRY

READING: Matthew 11: 25 - 30

"Come to Me, all you who labour and are heavy laden, and I will give you rest."

MATTHEW 11:28

Everyone who faces bereavement, be it sudden or expected, ask themselves the question, 'Could I have done more for my loved one?' Often there is a sense of guilt and self examination. This is because the opportunity of ministering to the one, who has passed on, is over and there is a vacuum in the heart and in the family circle. Even those who have 'gone the extra mile' go through this self examination and wish they had done more.

The only way you can deal with this is to take your burden to the Lord. Such a load will only add to your grief and make the journey through your pain and loss more difficult. No doubt you did what you could and fitted your caring into an already busy schedule. Let go of such accusations and rest in the fact that you were able to help in some little way. It is only when you do this that you find peace and further work through your pain and loss.

A positive way to deal with such remorseful feelings, is to think of the occasions when you were there for your loved one; others shared in the caring too and your loved one knew that you cared.

Just let go of your guilt and allow God to bind up your broken spirit and lift the burden. It is too heavy for you to carry.

Let go of your burden at the foot of the Cross
Taste of the sweetness of freedom from guilt
Lay down your load, it's too heavy for you
Just let the Saviour your spirit, renew!

Prior to Christ's death on the Cross, he visited the home of Lazarus in Bethany and John records the beautiful story of Mary anointing the feet of Jesus and wiping His feet with her hair. It was just a simple act, but He commended it, and when Judas was critical, He rebuked him. Whatever simple acts of kindness you have done, prior to the death of your loved one, were special.

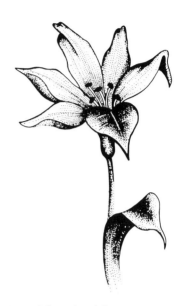

THE LILY

Consider the lily
so pure and so white:
With stem tall and slender,
flower dazzling bright!
In sunshine or shadow
the lily's arrayed
in more glory than
Solomon ever displayed!

Consider the lily,
she toils not, nor spins:
When grown, her mouth opens
to praise God and sing!
With no trace of worry
her potential she'll reach:
While growing and blooming
a sermon she'll preach!

Consider the lily
when robbed of your poise
by external pressures -
the world's bustle and noise.
Remember, her glory
came not from hard toil,
but just in accepting
new life from the soil!

DAY 6

TALK ABOUT YOUR GRIEF

READING: John 11: 1 - 16

"Now Jesus loved Martha and her sister and Lazarus.

"So, when He heard that he was sick, He stayed two more days in the same place where He was."

JOHN 11: 6 & 7

Jesus knew what was happening, so why did He delay? No doubt, He saw beyond the death to the resurrection of Lazarus. Jesus knew, His delay would bring more glory to God. Perhaps it was also to give the friends, gathered in the Bethany home, time to talk together. There had been a mourning period and Lazarus was four days in the tomb when Jesus arrived. His delay was not an accident, it was purposeful planning! He is always a step ahead of us!

Usually it does help to talk about the circumstances leading up to the death and to recall the good memories of the loved one.

Joan Wilson, from Enniskillen who lost daughter Marie, son Peter and husband Gordon, has written about her experience in her book, "All Shall be Well."

Joan found comfort in talking to others and reading about others who had passed through similar grief. She also found help in remembering the good times spent together, the stories, the jokes, and their favourite food - the thousand and one things that bound their lives together!

Your family and friends want to talk and have memories to share. Before long you will relive highlights from the past and together be helped by memories. You will laugh again! You will repeat sayings and imagine you can hear a voice from the past as scene after scene is relived through conversation and viewing photographs.

MEMORY

Memory brings a falling tear,
you bravely try to hide
behind a smile and face the world
as year follows year.
Down memory lane, you walk alone,
for others soon forget
the one whose memory will remain
with you 'till life's sunset!

Memory brings a surge of joy -
you smile, when you recall
the fun you had, the tricks you played,
the good days and the bad!
Fond memories are engraved by love –
of life, they form a part!
Nothing can ever them erase –
they're stamped upon the heart!

Memory is a priceless gift:
it helps to ease the pain
of human loss and loneliness
when death takes someone dear!
the mind becomes a gallery
of pictures set in gold,
valued by the owner
and never can be sold!
They are the greatest treasure
of all life's earthly store:
remembrance is the viewing time:
sorrow and joy the door!

DAY 7

A FRIEND WHO WILL NEVER FAIL

READING: Proverbs: 18:24

"… there is a friend who sticks closer than a brother."

PROVERBS 18:24

The Bible introduces us to some of the most beautiful human friendships, such as the bonds of friendship between Jonathan and David. It is recorded of Abraham that 'he was the friend of God'. In the New Testament we read of a wonderful friendship between the Virgin Mary and Elizabeth when both women faced a mutual problem and new future.

Luke 1:39 & 40.

"Now Mary arose in those days and went into the hill country with haste, to the city of Judah, and entered into the house of Zachariah and greeted Elizabeth."

It is obvious that this was a memorable visit for both women. Mary would have benefited greatly from being able to share her secret with another woman. The public disgrace of giving birth to a child out of wedlock would have weighed heavily on Mary's heart as she 'kept these things and pondered them in her heart'. At last she was able to talk to her cousin, Elizabeth!

You will need friends. Share your sorrow with a close friend – perhaps someone who has gone through a similar experience, but above all, share your sorrow with your Saviour. He will be there when others have gone for 'He is a friend who sticks closer than a brother'. He is always by your side and will not leave you in your hour of need.

Your Christian friends are praying for you and your greatest friend is by your side. He whispers, 'You are Mine'.

You Are Mine

To be the Lord's, when billows
hurl their angry blows:
To be the Lord's, and in life's darkest hour
His mercy know
is more than gold or jewel rare;
for this is love beyond compare:
I lay me down in peace content –
No enemy with purpose bent
can thwart the plan of God for me –
for I am His!

To be the Lord's, when waters deep
the soul destroy –
To be the Lord's, when every hope
is fading fast and cares annoy,
is wealth beyond our dream –
and so when every hope would seem
to be dying like a wounded dove –
God reveals His constant love –
Says, 'You are Mine'!

DAY 8

HEAVEN – GOD'S DWELLING PLACE

Reading: John 14: 1 - 6

"In My Father's house there are many mansions…"

JOHN 14:2

In my teens when I discovered God was my heavenly Father, I read numerous books about Heaven, my eternal destiny. It made me long to go there! Some time later, a number of my close friends died and that made me want to glean all the information I could on the place Jesus told us He was going to prepare.

I read a little book about the glories of Heaven that whetted my appetite more for my final destination.

The story was about a woman called Pam in California who was diagnosed with terminal cancer and was told she had probably just about one month to live. As a Christian she accepted God's will and decided to make the most of the time left to her by discovering what heaven would be like, as well as prepare to leave her husband plenty of frozen meals in the freezer.

She bought a little green recipe box with cards for her favourite recipes, but instead of writing recipes on the cards, she wrote Bible verses about heaven. Her close friends joined her in the search, so her recipe box filled up quite quickly.

Pam made a choice! She decided that if she were going on holiday she would read up all she could about her destination, therefore if she was going to heaven – never to return, she would like to know more about it!

What a wise decision! Pam had no fear of the future, so positively used her time to prepare to die. She shared her discoveries with a doctor friend and asked that he continue the study when the Lord took her home. You can imagine that little recipe box became a special treasure and a loving memory of Pam, to her respected friends!

A Distant Horizon

I see on yon horizon God's final resting place:
I forward press towards it,
redeemed by Sovereign Grace:
I see on yon horizon, people from every race
they look upon the Saviour - gaze upon His face!
On earth they sought His mercy and found in
Him their stay:
Earth's rugged paths behind them -
in Christ they found the way!

I see on yon horizon, Messiah, King of Kings
God of all creation, to whom all beings sing -
their song is one of worship
their praise is from the heart:
their joy now knows no limit,
for they know it's just the start
of all the hope they treasured while pilgrims on
this earth
and trust that you will follow to join them in
their mirth!

DAY 9

THERE IS HELP

READING: Psalm 121: 1-8

"I will lift up my eyes to the hills
From whence comes my help?
My help comes from the Lord,
Who made heaven and earth."

PSALM 121: 1;2

Perhaps you have had a week of dark and lonely nights and you are reading this and feel those nights will never end. Like David, who lamented,

"My tears have been my food day and night". Psalm 42:3

At this stage of your grief, there are no easy answers. It may help you to know that there are organisations, such as 'Care in Crisis' and 'Grief Share', who specialise in counselling the bereaved. They are skilled in this field: many of them, having been through difficult circumstances themselves, emerged with a desire to help others. Because of the help they received, they have undergone training and further study to help the bereaved.

Don't try to cope alone; you need others to share your burden; others whom you feel you can trust.

I received a letter from Elizabeth that brought fresh challenge and inspired me to continue writing. Elizabeth's husband was a tireless worker for the good of others. He died leaving Elizabeth a young widow with three small children. She was a teacher by profession so, after her husband's death, she faced many changes, including applying for a teaching post. Because her house was part of her husband's job, his death necessitated moving.

God helped his child to cope with all the trauma and today at eighty-five years of age she is sharing her experience with others.

It is my prayer that you will be able to trace the hand of a loving heavenly father, even though you do not understand what his plans are, and cannot fathom the mystery of suffering and death.

When Corrie ten Boom lost her sister in a Nazi concentration camp, she found a ministry in writing and speaking about her experience. Corrie is safely Home, but her books still encourage and help others cope with the pain of sorrow.

Her testimony to forgiving the person, who was responsible for her sister's death, when they met after the war, was a beautiful insight into the character of this woman, who knew God in a very intimate manner.

One of her favourite poems was the beautiful poem The Weaver.

A copy of the poem was given to me by her great niece when I visited "The Hiding Place", in Harlem.

The Weaver

My life is like a Weaving
Between my God and me,
I do not choose the colours:
He worketh steadily!
Of times he worketh sorrow
And I, in foolish pride
Forget he sees the upper
And I, the underside.

Not 'til the loom is silent
And shuttles cease to fly
Shall God unroll the canvas
And explain the reason why
The dark threads are as needful
In the Weaver's skilful hand
As the threads of gold and silver
In the pattern He has planned.
By Grant Tuller

DAY 10

THE HILL OF RECOVERY

READING: Psalm 34: 6 – 10

"The eternal God is your refuge and
underneath are the everlasting arms."
DEUTERONOMY 33:37

Recovery is a hill to climb and the path is difficult. You will
feel the chill of loneliness, the cold of isolation, the numbness
of disbelief; you will doubt the presence of the Good Shepherd.
But do remember, He is there, despite your feelings. He was
with your loved one, He carried your loved one through the
Valley of the Shadow of Death and He wants to carry you. He
whispers, "The eternal God is your refuge and underneath are
the everlasting arms."

He asks you to trust Him, even though you cannot see how
you will be able to rise above your grief and start to climb
again. If your loved one could speak to you, the words would
be reassuring: perhaps the message would be – 'go on; you'll
make it through this valley! Start climbing again! God has a
future for you and we shall meet again!'

In John chapter ten, we are introduced again to the theme of
the Shepherd. John reminds us that Jesus gave His life for the
sheep. This brings tremendous comfort to the sorrowing. Jesus
cared so much for us that He gave His life for the sheep.
Because of that, you can be assured that in your valley, He is
with you and will not fail to bring you through.

When my friend lost her child, she said to me…

"The Lord knows, I could not bear the severe pain all the time, so He graciously lifts the burden."

The pain will return, and time and time again you will have to climb the "Hill of Recovery", but the Lord will not ask you to bear more than you can carry.

Tears and Joy

Grief pierces the heart
like an arrow on target to kill:
It brings in its wake
pain and sorrow –
an emptiness nothing can fill!
But tears are the language of sorrow
expressing the heart's inner grief,
then cleansing and healing emotions –
restoring, and bringing relief.

Joy gladdens the heart
like a bird released from its cage –
It breaks into song –sometimes laughter:
dispels gloominess, sorrow or rage!
Tears can be the language of gladness,
expressing a freedom from care –
or in sharing life's blessings with others –
tears help us our hearts to make bare!

DAY 11

HOW WILL I FACE ANOTHER DAY?

READING: Psalm 28: 6 - 9

"As your days, so shall your strength be..."

DEUTERONOMY 33:25b

You thought it would become easier, but instead it seems to become harder. You were carried along by the support of family and friends during the last moments of your dear one's life and over the days prior to the funeral. There were so many people to talk to and so much to think about. Now the finality of what has happened is slowly sinking in and you feel you cannot face another day. You can, my friend, with the Lord's help!

There will be many times when you reach rock bottom. You will feel there is no way forward.

Easter can be particularly difficult for the bereaved. Because it is a time to reflect on the death of the Lord Jesus Christ and we follow the Biblical story through the Garden of Gethsemane to Golgotha. We follow the women to the grave, as they went with their spices to anoint the body of the Saviour. We feel his followers will never rise from the events of the Cross! But the resurrection changes everything! Jesus Christ has risen from the dead and is alive. The words of the two men who appeared to the women,

"Why look for the living among the dead? He is not here, He has risen!"

These words must have brought reassurance to all!

Christians believe in the "resurrection of the body", and you can be assured that your loved one will rise from the dead.

Very often the question is asked - "Will I know my loved one in heaven?"

Yes, the Bible makes it clear that we shall know our dear ones. Just as the disciples recognised Jesus, after the resurrection, so we shall know our loved ones.

Fresh Courage

I place my hand in Yours O Lord –
the way I cannot see:
My heart would fail, my strength is weak
so to Your arms I flee!

I ask for strength to cope with pain,
too much for me to bear!
I know there's help from God above
so hear my faintest prayer!

'My child, fear not to trust in Me'
I hear the Saviour say -
I bore the pain of Calvary
and know your pain today!

So with new courage
I will rise to brave the course ahead
and by the grace of God I'll feed
some hungry soul with 'bread'!

DAY 12

CARRYING MY GRIEF

READING: John 20: 11 -18

"...she turned round and saw Jesus standing there, and did not know that it was Jesus. Jesus said to her, 'Why are you weeping...'"

JOHN 20 14; 15

The circumstances leading up to bereavement differs for each of us. When the prognosis of a terminal illness is given and there is a predicted time scale of the life span, it is a very traumatic experience. Each individual deals with the news differently. One of the most difficult situations is to deal with the shock. For some the bereavement takes place the moment they receive the news: for others it seems as if the news does not register and hope continues until the actual moment of death.

You may be passing through two bereavements. Now that the loved one has actually passed away, you are coping with both the pain of the past and the more recent pain and loss of the physical death and funeral of a very special person.

Others are called on to nurse a loved one who has been immobile for a very long time. You too, suffer a double bereavement for you knew your loved one would never be the same, when you were given the diagnosis. Life changed for you drastically, and your recent bereavement has been made more difficult. Over a period of time, perhaps years, your life revolved around your loved one – you developed a routine and each day you coped with medical and other personnel calling at the home to alleviate your burden. Now all that has changed and you have to face a new future. You feel the pain and loneliness is unbearable.

Whatever the circumstances leading up to the 'Home-call' of your dear one, God knows all you have been through already and comes to you today with the reassurance of His Grace – It will be sufficient for today and all your tomorrows. It will not be easy, but with the prayers and help of others, you will come through. There are those who have been through a similar experience and may be able to help you by sharing their experience. Do seek help from others, but come to the One who is waiting to pour in His soothing balm. The wound is raw, but He understands and there is no situation too difficult for Him. Let Him help you through your pain today! Claim His promise -

"I will never leave you, or forsake you."

Hebrews 13:5

Christ is King

Do not cry: O do not cry;
Although the Saviour is to die:
Weep no more; O weep no more
for He will open heaven's door!
Sigh no more: O do not sigh -
Behold redemption draweth nigh!
Jesus will the victory win
-over sin!

Lift your eyes: O lift your eyes:
"It is finished!" The Saviour cried!
He arose: O He arose!
He triumphed over all His foes:
Joy at last: O joy at last!
The curse and wrath of God are past:
Sin and death have lost their sting
- Christ is King!

DAY 13

JOY COMES IN THE MORNING

READING: 1 Thessalonians 4:13 - 18

> "But I would not have you ignorant brethren, concerning those who have fallen asleep, lest you sorrow as others who have no hope."
>
> **THESSALONIANS 4:13**

One cannot explain the depth of sorrow and grief that accompanies the departure of another and nobody can fully enter into the pain of another, for every loss affects the individual differently. Some wish to bear their grief in silence; others want to talk about the events that led up to the death and the actual passing of the loved one; there are those who want to express their grief by relating incidents from the life of the deceased by which they will be remembered. It is important that each person who grieves is given the opportunity to work through the process, while friends and family give support and at the same time, allow space to grieve in the manner appropriate.

Death is something that we all must face at some time and is the natural outcome of life. The pain we experience is because we have developed a bond with another that has enriched our lives. What a priceless treasure! It is a gift from God and something that money can't buy.

There is the other aspect of death that brings relief. Prior to the funeral, we still have the earthly remains of our dear one and we could be tempted to think of the pain and grief as being mutual, but our pain is for ourselves; it is our loss that brings grief, for the loved one does not know or feel the pain. It is therefore good to remind ourselves that for the Christian, who has died as a member of God's family - Joy comes in the morning!

Our sorrow is in the earthly parting and for ourselves, but our hope is in a glorious resurrection from the dead, when "the dead will be raised incorruptible". When Christ comes back for His church, Paul tells us…

"…And the dead in Christ will rise first.

"Then we who are alive, and remain, shall be caught up together with them in the clouds to meet the Lord in the air. And thus we shall always be with the Lord." 1 Thessalonians 4: 16; 17

"Forever, with the Lord- Amen!

"So let it be!"

The following poem was written in the late nineteenth century, by a Bangor man, Charles W. Lepper…

Bereavement

The world is full of sorrow,
of suffering, grief, and pain;
But soon a bright tomorrow
Will cheer our hearts again!
We cannot help our tears,
We can't but mourn our loss,
But soon through endless years
We'll glory in the Cross!

The Cross of Jesus ended
Our deepest sorrow here -
And God the Father sends us
The Comforter to cheer!
Then let us sing His praises,
Though now we can't explain
His dealings here amaze us
But He will make it plain.

We'll trust Him though He slay us,
We'll trust through darkest days,
His Holy Word will stay us
And fill our hearts with praise.
Soon comes the golden morrow,
This night of gloom all past –
Then joy instead of sorrow;
His 'bairns' all Home at last!

DAY 14

LIFE IS A JOURNEY

READING: Psalm 23

"Yea though I walk through the valley
of the shadow of death…"

PSALM 23: 1

Life is a journey. We are all travelling on the road called 'life'
and one day it will end at the destination of death.

Imagine you are driving along a country road in late
September or early October. The day is chilly but bright. The
scene changes as you turn a corner and the road looms ahead.
It is straight as far as the eye can see until it narrows to a
point and is lost to the eye. As autumn lays her chilly hand on
nature, the green foliage is replaced with dazzling shades of
gold, rust, yellow, and brown; the foliage of the tree-lined
verges meets overhead and forms a natural tunnel. The road
dips and you experience the pleasure of a tunnel with a
difference. Instead of the blackness of night, there is the
brightness of day as shafts of autumn sunshine light up the
tunnel. There is hope in this tunnel!

At this stage in your grief, you will begin to experience the
shafts of light and sunshine in your tunnel of pain. You will
remember those happy occasions when you shared such
pleasures together. No doubt you will experience similar
feelings as you move slowly forward. The rays of sunshine will
quickly disappear and the tunnel will darken; farther along

the same thing will happen – such is the pain and joy of grief! David's wonderful Psalm does not cease to bring comfort to those who suffer the loss of loved one. It is a walk, not a drive, we commence.

"Yea though I walk through the valley of the shadow of death…" Grieving is a slow process and sometimes you will feel you have gone back a few paces. That is not the case! You can experience emotions of sadness, pleasure, remorse, shock and joy for short periods and change almost immediately. For example, a son or daughter may be depressed one moment, having lost a parent, and the sight of photograph with a smiling face can bring pleasure. Talking to a friend about a family holiday or some joyful experience can lift the spirits and bring a surge of happiness. As you walk through the valleys of grief and climb the difficult hills of bereavement, you are not alone. Others have travelled the same road and found their way.

You will carry your memories until you come to the same valley. Remember, He will be there too and will walk with you through the valley of the shadow of death. What consolation it brings to the child of God to have the assurance that we shall meet on the other shore. Be assured, God never breaks a promise! He placed a rainbow in the sky as a promise to the whole human race that He would never again destroy the world with a flood. Did He keep His promise? Of course He did and He will keep His promise to you.

Unchanging Love

Unchanging love –
when my feelings would say,
there's no purpose or plan
In what happened today:
the sorrow and heartache
through which I have passed
means God has forsaken –
your cause will be lost!
But His promise assures me
Of unchanging love
So I'll trust God, my Father
And rest in His love!

DAY 15

THE FINAL VICTORY

READING: Revelation: 21: 1-8

"And God will wipe away every tear from their eyes;..."

REVELATION 21:4

In the book of Revelation, we read of the exalted Lamb/ Shepherd. Here we visualise God's Throne with the Lamb at the centre as the Shepherd figure. There is no mistake as to who this is, for John makes it clear that He is ...

"The Lamb slain from the foundation of the world - He is the eternal "Word".

John writes in the first chapter of his gospel…

"In the beginning was the Word and the Word was God and the Word was with God, the same was in the beginning with God."

John 1:1

He is the Lamb typified in the Exodus of the Children of Israel from Egypt. When God was going to deliver His people from the bondage of Egypt under Pharaoh, He told Moses to instruct the Children of Israel to sprinkle the blood of a lamb on the lintels of the doors and when the angel of death would pass in the night, they would be protected. Jesus became the Lamb slain for the remission of the sins of the world.

He is the Lamb symbolised in the Wilderness. When the Children of Israel were bitten by a snake, Moses was instructed to place a bronze snake on a pole and those who looked to it were cured.

He was lifted up on the Cross and shed His blood for the Salvation of the World.

He is the Lamb who will lead all who believe in Him and trust Him through the valley of the shadow of death and then as the exalted Lamb/Shepherd, He will lead us to those eternal springs of Living Water! If He is going to lead us to springs of Living Water, we will still be following Him as the Shepherd for all eternity. What a prospect! What a plan! What a privilege to be part of the family of God!

Those springs will never dry up, and forever we shall be discovering the wonders of God's heaven – His "New Jerusalem," as described for us in the opening verses of Revelation, 21.

John tells us that we will not hunger or thirst any more and there shall be no more crying.

In the mean time there are tears. Grief and sorrow come to us all and shatter our homes, leaving us with a vacant chair. But be assured we will meet again in 'that land that is fairer than day'!

Until that day, remember your Christian friends are praying for you in your loss and the Saviour is praying for you. May you find courage to keep going until the day when God shall wipe away all tears!

"They shall neither hunger anymore nor thirst anymore; ... for the Lamb who is in the midst of the centre of the throne will Shepherd them and will lead them to living fountains of waters."

Revelation 7:16 ;17

Death is the last bridge over which you will tread and providing you're ready, you've nothing to dread –

your spirit will quietly cross to God's Home so don't be afraid when you hear Him say, 'Come'!

DAY 16

RELIEF THROUGH TEARS

READING: Psalm: 27

"Hear O Lord when I cry with my
voice…"

PSALM: 27:7

When is it right to cry? Cry when your emotions tell you.
Don't restrict your tears, for it makes the pain harder to bear!

Each of us will react differently. For example, the last
Christmas together brings joy to one and sadness to another.
A familiar laugh of a relative brings memories of a holiday
spent in the sun, and the tears flow.

Someone has described crying, when death claims a dear one,
as…

"Crying is love and hope staying alive in memory," so give
vent to your emotions and do not feel embarrassed. Your
friends will understand and may just quietly stay by your side
and whisper words of encouragement or leave you to deal with
your emotions. They want to sympathise with you but don't
know how to express their feelings. If they have not
experienced grief, they cannot help you, but will silently pray
for you.

"The Lord is my light and my Salvation
Whom shall I fear:
The Lord is the strength of my life
Of whom shall I be afraid?"
Psalm 27:1

Don't be afraid to cry, it will release pent up tensions and help relieve some of the pain. Let God's love flow through you to refresh and strengthen you for the days and weeks ahead. Your wound is still very raw and needs bathing in the tears of grief.

God Knows

Behind a smiling face,
there often is a care:
Oh, heavy heart bowed down with grief:
God listens to your prayer.
Your lips may never move
and no one see your tears:
Those inward pangs the Master sees:
He knows your hidden fears.

So trust His power today:
He does remember you!
Your name's engraved upon His hands:
Your spirit, He'll renew.

DAY 17

GRIEF AND PRAISE

READING: Psalm 97

"Oh come let us sing unto the Lord."
PSALM: 97:1

As healing comes, you will discover new truths. You will begin to connect pleasure with pain, as God heals your broken heart.

Because of the depth of your grief, you have discovered that no earthly friend could bring healing and deep comfort. In gratitude, you will begin to thank Him for His love and goodness. It is one of the miracles of God's healing touch. He knows that you cannot bear the pain all the time and has promised that if you ask Him, He will carry your burdens. When the realisation of this truth dawns, praise fills the heart and with the millions who have experienced God's healing touch, you begin to come to terms with the reality of life and death.

The Bible brings assurance to the believer that, "neither life nor death can separate us from the love of God which is in Christ Jesus" and expressions of gratitude fill the human heart.

There are those who have experienced joy and thankfulness that their loved one was taken without a more prolonged illness, or taken from a poor quality of life - in God's providence. Others are grateful for the strength they found to cope with the unexpected, after the initial shock and disbelief of their loss. This does not take away from the sadness and pain, but can bring healing in the knowledge that God has a plan for each life.

There is a bright tomorrow!

Fresh Courage

God's grace is sufficient for my every need:
Whatever the future, I know He will lead
so trusting His promise, I'll conquer my fear,
in the eye of the storm, my Captain will steer.

The path You have brought me, was meant for my good
so Lord give the strength to conquer all moods:
I pray You will help me, fresh courage to claim
to live for Your Kingdom – Let this be my aim!

Then like my loved one, I'll turn the last bend,
to heaven and Home my soul will ascend!
No parting; no sorrow, on yon blissful shore;
no dying; no crying, for evermore!

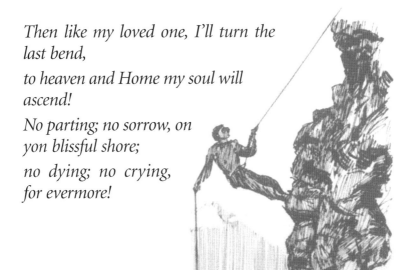

DAY 18

THE BEAUTY OF SILENCE

READING: Luke 2:

"But Mary kept all these things and
pondered them in her heart".

LUKE 2:19

When the angel revealed to Mary that she would bring to birth
the Saviour of the world, we read that Mary did not discuss
the revelation with anyone, but kept it a secret. When we are
in turmoil, it is not easy to keep quiet, but sometimes, silence
brings poise and healing.

In bereavement, we experience all kinds of emotions. There
will be times when we want to talk as well as moments when
we want to be alone. How good it is to have someone near
when we want to talk! In the quietness of your grief offer a
silent prayer and ask God to bring you the right people for
your particular need, those with whom you can share your
thoughts. Remember, many of your friends are praying for
you and sometimes they don't know what to say. You may be
tempted to think they don't care, but they do and long to be
there for you.

Your friends want you to feel the strength of God's love, so as
they pray, allow God to minister to you. There is a beauty in
silence and when that silence is broken, a "word fitly spoken
is like apples of gold in pictures of silver" – It is meaningful
and precious!

When God is Silent

When God is silent, do not fear –
He's just a prayer away
and waits to chase the dark of night
and bring a bright new day!

He whispers, words of hope to you
'I'm with you in your pain
I understand the grief you bear -
intended for your gain!

Your loved one now has left this scene
Because I beckoned – Come!
The time had come to leave earth's ties
and hear My 'Welcome Home!'

DAY 19

TIME FOR REFLECTION

READING: Matthew 26: 6 – 13

"The memory of the righteous is blessed…"

PROVERBS 10:7

To deal adequately with grief, there needs to be times of reflection. This can be both helpful and painful.

One of the best ways of dealing with grief is to think of the legacy of the life of the one you loved: their influence on your life and on the lives of others. Did their living change you in any way? Gradually, you will realise that it was because of what they did and what they said that made them so special. There was something about them that was different! Not only has the physical part of that special person gone, but their influence.

In your time of reflection, thank God for how the person changed you and ask God to help you take advantage of their impact, so that you too will be missed when you are taken from us. This should be a positive step towards healing. Your loved one's memory will not be wiped out, because it is written on your heart, but their contribution to your life has made a difference and by God's grace, you will seek to build on that.

The proverb, "Actions speak louder than words!" is very often true in life, but certainly after death, it is absolutely true.

A grandmother grieved over the death of her grandchild. When asked what she would miss most, there was no hesitation in her reply.

"I have all the memories of her childhood, when together we grew in love, and in understanding family bonds. Growing from childhood to womanhood, when she became even closer and told me about the boyfriends. Most of all, I will miss her weekly visits to me. Those visits were not rushed, for she took time with her elderly 'Gran' to talk and tell me what she had been doing – she kept me up-to-date with all the family news, when others were busy."

If 'Gran' needed anything, she knew there was someone at the other end of the telephone who would bring it on her next visit.

Such commitment expresses love and appreciation. There was no generation gap, but a loving devotion to a very special 'Gran'.

Grateful

I Thank God for love and friendship
for kind words and thoughtful deeds
I know I won't forget the way
such love kept shining through:
although I'll miss the friendship;
I'll cherish all the seeds -
ask God to help me plant them
by my actions, words and deeds!

A little seed can bloom into a flowering plant!

DAY 20

HEAVEN IS MY ETERNAL HOME

READING: Revelation. 22: 1-6

"And there shall be no more curse, but the throne of God and of the Lamb shall be in it, and His servants shall serve Him."

REVELATION: 22;3

Very often, people ask, 'What shall we be doing in heaven?' We do not fully know but the Scriptures give us an insight occasionally. We know we will be serving, so we shall be active: there will be worship and adoration of the Saviour: we shall know one another in heaven, and we know there will be no pain, and sorrow will be no more.

John gives us a beautiful insight into the relaxation of heaven and records,

"He showed me a pure river of water of life, clear as crystal, proceeding from the throne of God and of the Lamb."

I love to watch the river in its changing moods and this will give me untold pleasure. Time will be no more, so we shall not be rushing around and will have time to enjoy everything. This river will be different to all others for there is no dirt or grim collected as it flows. The dirt and grim of sin has been removed from God's new heaven and we shall enjoy the cleanliness.

Rest content today, knowing that your loved one has crossed the chilling river of death and we shall join the multitude, from all nations and all ages, to see the Saviour and enjoy the pure river of life.

The Apostle John's description of heaven assures us there will be no separation: the distance now brings pain and heartache for we no longer see the face of the one we loved.

"There will be no more sea…"

Sea speaks of distance and separation, but the picture of this river, is one to bring enjoyment by its beauty and purity, not to separate.

Dawn

As God rolls back the mantle of night,
bringing the first rays of sun into sight:
As from its slumber all nature awakes
so the first note of the dawn chorus breaks:
each bird chirps its own melodious song,
then drifts into harmony; before very long
the air is filled with a volume of praise,
while to the Creator their anthem they raise.

When God rolls back sin's mantle of night
and to my conscience the Spirit brings light:
as from its slumber my dead soul awakes;
through all my nature a melody breaks
to Jesus my Saviour, to whom I belong -
my voice joins all nature in jubilant song -
You came from the Glory, sinners to save
and triumphed victorious over the grave!

When God rolls back earth's mantle of night
and Christ descends in great splendour and light:
then from its slumber the world He awakes,
as from the four corners the redeemed ones He
takes:
Oh what a moment, by the Church waited long
when we shall be raptured - the resurrection
morn!
Loved ones united, together to gaze
on the face of the Saviour - forever to praise!

DAY 21

TRYING TO FIND ANSWERS

READING: Mark 4:35 - 41

"Teacher, do You not care that we are
perishing?"

MARK 4: 38

The tempest was raging on the Sea of Galilee and Jesus was
asleep in the boat. Did He not care? Of course He cared! He
was with them in the boat and when it was necessary, He
stepped into the situation and calmed the storm.

After the tragedy of bereavement has rocked our frail boat,
we ask questions. Where was the Master? Why did my loved
one die? Could I have done more? You tried to do your best
but you felt helpless. You did not want to face the possibility
of losing your dear one. 'Where there's life, there's hope', you
thought, as you learned to cope with each day. You watched
with an ache in your heart, refusing to believe that one day it
would come to an end. You try to find consolation!

Was there anything I could have done that would have
changed the outcome? You ask yourself question after
question, but no answers are forthcoming. You are faced with
the choice of trusting God or allowing bitterness to creep in.

You will need time to adjust, but that will come in due course.
Don't set a time, but tell the Lord you are prepared to trust
Him to help you. You must not be concerned with trying to
please others by being brave. Let yourself cry! It is part of

grieving. Do not feel guilty, but allow the process of grieving to begin. Nobody can enter your secret world just now, only the One who knows the secrets of our hearts.

He Will Be With You

He will be with you in sunshine,
He will be with you in shade,
He still keeps His covenant promise –
He's Almighty, Eternal, I Am!
He gave to Moses His promise,
was faithful to him to the end
and He kept His promise to Joshua,
so, on God's faithfulness you can depend!

DAY 22

WHERE DO I GO FROM HERE?

READING: Psalm, 121

"I will lift up my eyes to the hills…"

PSALM 121:1

You must lift your eyes heavenward. Your help to face the future, comes from the Lord who made heaven and earth. The way forward is to take the first step, knowing that "He will not suffer your foot to be moved."

I pour out my grief at the Master's feet;
Broken in spirit, I seek His release!
He pours in His balm to my grief-stricken heart
then binds up the wound
and gives me a new start!

At this stage you cannot see a future, but God has a plan for your life and He will help you pick up the threads. Your friends are praying for you that you will be able to at least take steps towards new horizons. God wants to help you and your friends too want to help you. Call your friends on the phone when you feel you want to talk to someone. Don't battle alone because you will fight a losing battle. There are no easy answers to your grief but treasure your memories and walk down the corridors of memory. Remember the things that brought you happiness. You may not be able to look at photographs just yet – that may be too painful. For some people it takes years before they can look at a picture of their loved one, but for others, photos bring back the happiness and pleasure of the company of the one they mourn.

Memory

Memory brings a falling tear, you bravely try to hide
behind a smile and face the world as year follows year.
Down memory lane, you walk alone,
for others soon forget the one whose memory
will remain with you, till life's sunset!

Memory brings a surge of joy -
you smile, when you recall
the fun you had, the tricks you played,
the good days and the bad!
Fond memories are engraved by love –
of life, they form a part!
Nothing can ever them erase –
they're stamped upon the heart!

Memory is a priceless gift: it helps to ease the pain
of human loss and loneliness
when death takes someone dear!
the mind becomes a gallery of pictures set in gold,
valued by the owner and never can be sold!
They are the greatest treasure
of all life's earthly store:
remembrance is the viewing time:
sorrow and joy the door!

DAY 23

GOD HAS A 'BLUE PRINT' FOR MY LIFE!

READING: Jeremiah 1: 1 – 19

"Before I formed you in the womb I knew you…"

JEREMIAH 1: 5a

The prophet Jeremiah was not prepared for God's plan for his life. When God spoke to him, he said,

"Ah, Lord God!

"I cannot speak,

"For I am a youth…" Jeremiah 1:6

God had to speak forcibly to Jeremiah. He gently rebukes him for his excuses and shows him that He would send him to the people.

God has a purpose for each one of us. Like a jigsaw puzzle, the pieces are all there, but the finished work will only be viewed, on completion. Like a tapestry, God is working on our lives to prepare us for His heaven and when the tapestry is complete, He will call us Home. At the moment we can only see the under side but when the upper side is revealed, we shall see that even the moment of our departure from time into eternity had been part of His perfect plan.

No doubt, you can look back to childhood and see how God was preparing you for the future. You did not see it then, but in hindsight, there was a purpose in the events of your life, that you did not foresee!

Longfellow, in his Psalm of Life, wrote…

"Lives of great men all remind us
We can make our lives sublime,
And, departing, leave behind us
Footprints on the sands of time:-
"Footprints, that perhaps another,
Sailing o'er life's solemn main,
A forlorn and shipwrecked brother,
Seeing, shall take heart again
"Let us then, be up and doing,
With a heart for any fate;
Still achieving, still pursuing,
Learn to labour and to wait."

Whether you are a housewife or a public figure, God is bringing you through a new experience and out, of the ashes of sorrow, He will… work all things together for good!

This moment in time was in God's divine plan for you. The one, whose parting you mourn, was planned by a loving God. All you shared together and all your dreams, God knew about them – and He knows the future. You would have liked that you had been the one to go first, but that was not in His plan.

He has given you the gift of life and it is a special treasure to invest for eternity. Your loved one would want you to carry on, so place your hand in the hand of God and go into the future. Be assured that your loved one was called Home in God's time and although you cannot understand it now, you will understand it in eternity.

'God will roll back the canvas and explain the reason why'!

Footprints on the Sands of Time

Let me leave footsteps on the sand of time
that others may see, and some purpose find!
Help me not cherish some illusive dream
but serve Christ Jesus, the lone Nazarene.

Let me leave footprints in the sands of time
for short is the life span that I can call mine!
Soon I shall leave for realms of the blest –
May others who walk in my footsteps be blessed!

Let me leave footprints in the sands of time
that others will see as a heavenward sign –
guiding to Jesus, God's only Son
Who willingly trod the winepress alone!

DAY 24

FACING DEATH WITH CONFIDENCE

READING: 1 Corinthians 15:50 – 58

"O Death, where is your sting? O Hades, where is your victory?"

CORINTHIANS 15:55

In the twenty-first century, we are caught up in a world of science fiction. It is a fantasy world void of reality.

We must not imagine that we approach the subject of 'Life after Death' or 'Heaven' with the same mind set. Where do we go for a reliable resource to learn about death and face it without fear? The Bible is the only reliable and true resource we have; therefore we need to know what it teaches about death?

Because Jesus Christ faced death with confidence and showed us that the greatest enemy is sin and its consequences, we can face death without fear. He paid the price for our sin that we might stand before a Holy God, justified. He met the demands of divine justice, thus setting us free from the penalty of sin.

Writing to the church in Corinth, Paul explained that death was "falling asleep" in Christ. The hymn writer summed it up succinctly when he penned the beautiful words...

"When my spirit clothed immortal, wings its way to realms of day,

"This my song through endless ages, Jesus led me all the way!"

"Be like a bird that, halting in its flight,

rests on a bough too slight.

And feeling it give way beneath him

sings, knowing he hath wings."

Lettie Cowman

When my mother died, I had a sad but wonderful experience.

I was not present at the time, as I had gone home to bring a flask and some refreshments for my older sister and myself. We were told her death was not imminent, but it was arranged that some members of the family would stay.

I had brought home two garments to wash and had just put them into the spin dryer when the 'phone rang. I thought it was from the hospital to tell me to bring something else. It did not even enter my mind that it was to tell me my mother had died.

I jumped into the car, thinking there was a mistake, and I would still see her alive. As I lifted her lifeless hand and felt for a pulse, I knew her spirit had taken flight!

My older sister could see I was upset, and placing her arm around me, said, "Vera, it was beautiful, it was just like a little bird taking flight!"

DAY 25

SURVIVORS OF A SUICIDE

READING: Psalm 46: 1 - 13

"God is our refuge and strength,

"A very present help in trouble:

"Therefore we will not fear

"Even though the earth be removed

"And the mountains be carried into

the midst of the sea."

PSALM 46:1

Survivors of suicide want answers for themselves and from God to the many questions that flood their minds in trying to come to terms with their awful pain. Those who have prayed for their family find it difficult to accept the fact that God did not intervene to prevent it happening.

When the haze of disbelief lifts, very often there is a cry of lament and protest – "Why God?"

A mother who was the survivor of her child's suicide was haunted by two fears – the guilt of not getting her son to the doctor soon enough and the haunting thought the child could not cope with the life she gave him.

A father, whose teenage son took his own life, struggled with the double burden of grief and, what he termed, "the guilt and stigma attached to suicide."

"Could I have done something to prevent it?"

"Why was I not more observant to detect the mental conflict and struggles?"

Because God is silent and the answers given by others fail to bring assurance, the loved ones try to pick up the pieces and stumble into a future tarnished by guilt and fear. Nobody will ever be able to provide answers to the many conflicting questions of those who lose a loved one, through suicide. For some, the only solution is to conclude - parents are to blame. However, to the question of, "Are the parents (or some member of the family) to blame, we can turn to the healing of the blind man recorded in the gospels, for an answer.

The disciples of Jesus asked the question (John 9: 1 – 11).

"Master, who sinned, this man or his parents…?" (v1).

Jesus answered this by affirming that neither had the man or his parents sinned. It is interesting that Jesus did not give a third reason. He did not answer the question of suffering, grief and death.

Jesus gave release to the guilt aspect of blame. He made a statement that has comforted multitudes of guilt stricken mourners in every generation. It is particularly reassuring to the survivors of a suicide.

Many writers have tried to explain the mystery of pain, suffering and death, but here are no simple answers. When Adam and Eve sinned in the Garden of Eden, sickness, pain and death entered our world and unfortunately, we all bear the consequences of the fall of man, as recorded in the book of Genesis.

It may be early days, but you have a future that God wants you to look forward to with purpose and anticipation. It is possible to survive and emerge with an acceptance that brings peace and a release from guilt that determines a positive and satisfying future. You will go through the process of bereavement, you will still miss your loved one, but you can discover a loving Heavenly Father, either for the first time or a new intimacy that enables you to trust Him for the future.

God has promised to help you. He understands your questions when others have no satisfactory answers. He is not angry with you for your reaction and longs to bring you to a place of intimacy with Himself, as well as hope for the future.

Read Psalm 46; meditate on this beautiful Hebrew poem by David, the shepherd, poet and king, and you will find comfort and strength to face the future.

We can only see a little of the ocean
when we stand at the rocky shore
But out there, beyond the eye's horizon
there's more - there's more.
We can only see a little of God's loving
a few rich samples of His mighty store,
But out there, beyond the eye's horizon
there's more - there's more!

Author unknown

DAY 26

ETERNITY

READING: John 1: 1 - 12

"In the beginning was the Word, and
the Word was with God, and the
Word was God. The same was in the
beginning, with God."

JOHN 1: 1; 2

Because we are limited by the boundaries of time, it is difficult
for us to conceive the idea of timelessness. My late niece had
a favourite poem of mine that was published in 1985 in The
Smile of Truth. No matter how many poems I wrote, she
would always say, "My favourite is Eternity."

In the poem, I tried to capture something of the timelessness
of eternity - feeble though it may be it must have captured
Lynn's thoughts. She is now there, enjoying the immediate
presence of her Saviour and we can know with assurance, that
we will join her in "The Sweet bye and bye".

Eternity

When you have counted every grain
of sand from shore to shore:
Then climbed each hill and mountain peak
and lands beyond explored:
When you have dried all fallen tears,
mended each broken heart:
Of the countless years of eternity
it will only be the start.

When you have counted all the stars
of heaven from east to west,
and walked all roads and mountain trails
-yes, taking time to rest!
when you have brought a million smiles
to people, worlds apart;
of the countless years of eternity -
it will only be the start.

It will be worth it all when we see Jesus!

DAY 27
STRENGTHENED TO COPE WITH GRIEF

READING: Matthew 26: 36 – 46 & Luke 22: 43 & 44

"O My Father, if it is possible, let this cup pass from Me: nevertheless, not as I will, but as you will."

MATTHEW 26: 39

"So He left them, went away again, and prayed the third time, saying the same words."

LUKE 22: 43 & 44

Although there are those who have never questioned the will of God in the loss of a dear one, there are those who struggle in accepting their loss and do question God.

I asked a close friend, whose son died as a result of an accident

"Did you ever question God?"

Her son was a lively boy with a host of friends, he was athletic, had a sharp brain and friendly manner. He was a typical boy emerging into adolescence, with his sights set on achieving his goals.

As I thought of what my friend would miss by not seeing her son grow to manhood, her reply touched me greatly. She said she never questioned God, though the loss of her son was heart breaking.

You may have asked God for a reason; wondered why it should have happened to you – but there were no answers, only 'ifs' and 'buts' to ponder over! Afterwards, you may have felt a sense of guilt for questioning God.

To those who ask questions, it should bring reassurance to remember that Jesus questioned His Father in the Garden of Gethsemane…

"O My Father, if it be possible, let this cup pass from Me…" He repeated His request three times, but was willing to accept His Father's will…

"Nevertheless, not My will, but Yours be done."

Luke tells us that

"an angel appeared to Him from heaven, strengthening Him."

Luke 22:43.

In your times of questioning, remember, God knows your thoughts. He sees the depth of your grief! He comes today to strengthen you. Accept His strength, draw on His resources and claim His promises…

"The Lord is my strength and my shield:
My heart trusted in Him, and I am greatly helped:"

Psalm 28: 7a

"Let not your heart be troubled, you believe in God, believe also in Me."

John 14:1

Not Rejected

Not rejected -
the prayer of my heart:
When to God I drew near
with my turmoil and fear:
He heard my faint cry,
as to me He drew nigh:
Not rejected -
God answered my sigh!

Not rejected -
that longing for peace:
When my heart sighed for rest
and to be at my best,
He came like the dove
bringing comfort and love:
Not rejected -
in Heaven above

Not rejected -
My yearning to serve:
When I yielded my all
and I answered His call:
My joy was complete
and I fell at His feet:
Not rejected -
at the Mercy Seat.

DAY 28

HELPING YOU THROUGH GRIEF

READING: Psalm 62: 5 - 8

"Bear one another's burdens, and so
fulfil the law of Christ."

GALATIANS 6: 2

It is not God's will that you bear your burden alone, although grief is a very personal experience and most of us have battled through our deepest emotions, alone. Those who have travelled the lonely road of bereavement can help for they have known the pain of parting. If you have found a friend who understands, you will know the comfort it has brought to you. If you have not been able to share your intimate thoughts and feeling with another, ask God to bring the right person along who will understand and will lend a listening ear.

Accept the help of others in practical ways. It will take time for you to see through the maze of recent events, but as you face the future, you will need your friends.

Books can be a real source of comfort and help. Reading the right book can help you through moments of deep grief. As you enter another's mind, you can receive answers to your questions without having to voice your question, or without wondering if the person really understands your particular pain. You make new friends through reading, particularly books revealing how others coped with their grief. Your family and friends may not always be available but you can pick up a book at any time.

The best book to read is the Bible. The book of Psalms takes you into King David's world of pain, fear, turmoil and remorse when his son dies. The Psalms are full of sadness and encouragement and many find them a tremendous help in times of bereavement. The Gospels will take you to the house of morning – you will see how Jesus brought comfort to the sorrowing.

Care in Crisis and Grief Care are two organisations with trained dedicated counsellors and will give help if requested.

Tears and Joy

Grief pierces the heart
like an arrow on target to kill.
It brings in its wake, pain and sorrow -
an emptiness nothing can fill:
but tears are the language of sorrow,
expressing the hearts inner grief,
then cleansing and healing emotions,
restoring and bringing relief.
Joy gladdens the heart
like a bird released from its cage:
it breaks into song, sometimes laughter -
dispels gloominess, sorrow or rage.

Tears can be the language of gladness,
expressing a freedom from care -
or sharing life's blessings with others,
tears help us our hearts to make bare.

OUR FRIEND SLEEPS

READING: 1 Thessalonians 4: 13 & 18

"I do not want you to be ignorant, brethren, concerning those who have fallen asleep, lest you sorrow as others who have no hope."

I THESSALONIANS 4:13

In his letter to the church at Thessalonica, the Apostle Paul reminded his readers of the truth that death was not something to be dreaded, but was like falling asleep. He reiterated the truth Jesus taught the disciples gathered in the home of Mary, Martha and Lazarus, in Bethany. Referring to the deceased, Jesus said...

"Our friend Lazarus sleeps, but I go that I may wake him." John 11:11

The disciples were confused for they knew that Lazarus was not sleeping. Jesus wanted to teach His disciples a truth they would remember when He would rise from the dead. He declared to them plainly...

"Lazarus is dead." John 11:14

It was in this setting that Jesus makes one of the most profound statements about Himself...

"I am the resurrection and the life, he who believes in Me, though he may die, he shall live.

"And whoever lives and believes in Me shall never die..."

He then challenged Martha...

"Do you believe this?" John 11:25; 26.

Martha's response is immediate - "Yes, Lord, I believe that You are the Christ, the Son of God, who is to come into the world." John 11: 27

It is the same Jesus who comes to you today to assure you that your loved one is safely through the valley of the shadow of death and will one day be resurrected and join the heavenly choirs, singing...

"Unto Him who has loved us and washed us from sin:

"Unto Him be the glory forever, Amen!

Death

No sting in death!
for Jesus died
to deal with sin and give you peace
in Christ.
No sting in death!
so do not fear
to cross the vale and wake to be
with Christ.

No sting in death!
Just sleep my child
so close your eyes and you'll awake
in Heaven.

When Christ returns, a second time...

"...and the dead in Christ will rise first.

"Then we who are alive and remain shall be caught up together with them in the clouds to meet the Lord in the air. And thus we shall always be with the Lord."

1 Thessalonians 4: 16; 17

Day 30

A LAND 'FAIRER THAN DAY'

READING: Revelation 21: 1 - 8

"Now I saw a new heaven and a new earth, for the first heaven and the first earth had passed away. Also there was no more sea.

"Then I, John, saw the holy city, New Jerusalem, coming down out of heaven from God, prepared as a bride adorned for her husband."

REVELATION 21: 1; 2

When Adam and Eve sinned in the Garden of Eden, God not only put a curse on mankind, but he cursed the earth; thus we have weeds and thistles.

Why is it necessary to use pesticides on the land? Why do we suffer pain as a result of toiling in agriculture? Because sin entered into the world at The Fall - The results are endured by us all because we have inherited Adam's fallen nature. But thank God, Jesus Christ came and died an atoning death for us and made it possible for us to be forgiven and brought back into a right relationship with God. Such trust and faith in Christ, takes the sting out of death - we know we have hope beyond the grave and the great prospect of sharing God's new heaven and new earth!

Poets and writers have tried to describe it for over two thousand years, and all our words fail to depict its perfection and grandeur.

S. Fillmore Bennett wrote some of the most beautiful words to describe heaven. They have been quoted and sung by generations of aspiring Christians anticipating the glories of heaven...

"There's a land that is fairer than day
And by faith we can see it afar
And the Father waits over the way
to prepare us a dwelling place there!"

"In the sweet bye and bye
We shall meet on that beautiful shore
In the sweet bye
We shall meet on that beautiful shore."

The equally, beautiful music, written by J. Webster, with variations added by another musician, has challenged young musicians aspiring to heights of brilliance in playing the piano. The talented trio have produced a masterpiece!

God gave John a vision of the new heaven and the new earth when he was exiled on the Isle of Patmos for his faith. He describes it adequately for us to visualise a perfect environment, like the first Eden, without sin and suffering and beautifully adds - "there will be no more sea!" Sea speaks of separation, so this is a most comforting thought for us in our time of bereavement. There will be no separation from our loved ones, and above all we shall be with Christ our Saviour and Lord.

Ready

When the trumpet sounds
and the dead are raised
to meet the Lord in the air -
we too shall rise and go with Him
to the place He has prepared!

DAY 31

LOOKING BACK AND LOOKING FORWARD

READING: 2 Timothy 4: 6 - 22

" I have fought a good fight, I have finished the race. I have kept the faith."

2 TIMOTHY 4:7

The apostle Paul had reached the end of his journey. He writes a farewell to young Timothy for he knows he will soon be going Home to heaven. He is ready!

"...the time of my departure is at hand", writes Paul to his young companion. Despite the fact that Demas had forsaken him and, apart from Luke he was alone, he was triumphant as he reminds Timothy there is a crown of righteousness prepared for him, and for all who "have loved His appearing."

Looking back, he is grateful to the Lord for His protection and faithfulness and reaffirms his confidence in God's protection and deliverance. Looking ahead, he sees the goal before him – a crown of righteousness! He has kept on track and now he is going to his reward.

Before us, and by God's grace, let us endeavour to learn from his example and dedication.

No doubt, after the apostle of Paul went to be with Christ, there were many who looked back at his life and were thankful that he ever came their way. His missionary journeys had taken him to so many places and churches had been established. So many responded to the preaching of the Gospel under his ministry! There were countless individuals whose lives were changed because Paul obeyed God by responding to the call to repentance and faith on the Damascus road, and later, obeying the leading of the Holy Spirit to preach the Gospel.

We can look back in thankfulness for the lives of our loved ones, who have gone, and learn from their example. They can still influence us in our daily living by the memory of their love, and winsome ways. You have special memories because of the bonds between you. Now, although not present, they have left you something money cannot buy – a host of loving memories!

God lent a special person to you for a time -your life would have been poorer without that dear one, but enriched because you knew them in an intimate way. Now a chapter has closed and a new one has opened, with the knowledge and assurance that you will meet again.

Influence

I walked along a river bank:
threw in a pebble and it sank.
I watched the ripples multiply:
increase in strength, then spread and die!
How like the influence of our lives –
the ripples spread, man sees them stretch –
But when the soul and body part
influence makes a fresh new start
for only will the shores of time
break your influence and mine!

PART TWO

There are thirty one readings in the first part of Joy in the Morning. It is intended that this will cover the first month of your bereavement. Help is available through centres such as Care in Crisis and Grief Share. These organisations have trained personnel who will help you further and recommend helpful literature.

It is impossible to cover the subject of bereavement adequately without relating some real life stories of those who coped with grief and found a future after losing a loved one.

If I have not covered some aspect of your grief, I apologise, but there are other books dealing with more specific situations with which you could identify. Please do seek further help and don't try to bear your burden alone.

In introducing part two, I want to express my gratitude to those who gave me time and shared their pain and loss. I have to confess, it has been a very moving experience for me as I have shared the memories of those who have "walked through the valley of the shadow…" and parted with a dear one - who had to leave and walk alone through "the shadow of death".

No words can describe the grief and pain of the loss of a dear one. Each person has coped in different and amazing ways. For me, it has been a learning experience as I have tried to plumb the depths of grief, as well as sympathetically lend a listening ear. I feel privileged to be able to share with you my discoveries and trust that you will find comfort and perhaps some answers to your questions. With God's help, you too can cope, but constantly remembering…

"Not 'till the loom is silent
and the shuttle cease to fly
Will God unveil the canvas
and explain the reason – Why?"

CHILDREN AND GRIEF

At a time of bereavement, children can be forgotten about; sometimes they are left to discover the mysteries of life and death on their own. Nobody is to blame for it, but because adults are involved in the traumatic circumstances of the death of their loved one, children struggle with bewilderment and, not knowing the facts, they watch the reactions of the grown ups.

It is important to take time and make the necessary arrangements to protect them from emotional damage related to bereavement. They have to mourn the loss of their relative and in their innocence they look for help and there is none. Very often, because the parents are involved in the funeral arrangements, the children are left with friends or more distant relatives, who are their 'baby-sitters'. If they are allowed to be part of the funeral party, they have many questions to which they expect answers.

Why did Mummy leave the house so quickly? Why is Daddy so sad and doesn't want to talk? What is wrong with Granny? The questions are endless in a child's developing mind.

In a particular situation when a child wanted to stay for long periods in the room where Granny's remains lay in the coffin, he asked numerous questions. On the day of the funeral, he wanted to know why Granny didn't look the same as on the previous day. When the funeral procession was leaving the house and he was placed with a family member, farther away from the chief mourners, he requested to join them so that he could see the coffin being lowered into the grave at the cemetery.

How do we react in these circumstances? Obviously, if we are unprepared, mistakes can be made: mistakes that could leave a lasting scar on the mind of a sensitive child. Because children, like adults, react in different ways in a bereavement situation, we need to be aware of their needs and handle each tender 'plant' with care. In a brief reference to the subject of 'Children and Grief', it is not possible to give guidance as to how to deal with these little ones, but there are those skilled in handling the trauma of death as related to children, and would help you through your particular situation.

If through reading 'Joy in the Morning' readers become aware of the need to be more observant of children's needs in times of bereavement, it will have accomplished its goal. Help is available and there are excellent books available, both for parents and children.

LIFE CHANGES FOR A FAMILY

"As one of four children, we had a very happy childhood. Brought up on a farm, we enjoyed the freedom of the countryside and the opportunities to work together as a family doing the farm chores.

"My parents weren't Christians and they did not see the need to send us to church and Sunday school to learn the Word of God. On Sunday, we usually went to Newcastle for the day, and enjoyed a family picnic.

"When I was ten years old, my mother went into hospital for a routine operation. To cheer her up, we used our 'egg money' to buy her a milk jug, as a 'coming home' present.

"The operation went well and she started to recover. We couldn't wait until she came home!

"A few days later Daddy was urgently summoned to the hospital. We did not know at the time but Mummy's condition had suddenly deteriorated. Daddy remained at the hospital and kind neighbours had to come in to help us with the milking.

"The next morning when we went down to the byre to prepare for the first milking of the day, we discovered Daddy sitting on his milking stool with both milk and tears filling the bucket. He was sobbing uncontrollably; was unable to speak, when we asked him what was wrong.

"This was a scene, I shall never forget! The next thing I can remember was our minister arriving in the yard and bringing us down to our grandmother's house, the other house on the farm.

"There he broke the news to granny and four of us, aged twelve, ten, eight and six, that Mummy had 'passed away during the night.'

"My father and mother were well known in the area and many people came to pay their respects to Mummy. I clearly remember directing the cars as to where to park in our yard, during the days of the wake.

My father decided that we should not attend the funeral, so we stayed with one of our aunts.

"How would life ever be the same without Mummy? We were all too young to understand the full consequences of what had happened. Daddy started to lose interest in the farm and I had to stay off school to help with the milking.

"A few years later, we were to learn that Mummy had come to personal faith in the Lord Jesus Christ, through the ministry of a Hospital Visitor, Tommy Ryans. Unfortunately, Daddy blamed God for Mummy's death and his heart became hardened towards God and the Gospel message.

"Things became very difficult in the home. After much discussion with his sisters, but not with us, Dad decided to advertise for a 'live-in' housekeeper. He really was not coping with both farm chores and family life.

"A single girl from Donegal replied to his advertisement, and came to live with us, a few years after Mummy's death.

"'God works in a mysterious way, His wonders to perform.'

When she arrived, we discovered that she was a Christian. She sent us to Sunday school and started to bring Daddy and us to places where we would hear the Gospel. For the first time we heard the wonderful news that God loved us so much that He gave His Son to die for us.

"For God so loved the world that He gave His only begotten Son, that whosoever believes in Him, should not perish, but have everlasting life."

One by one, the four of us realised our need of a Saviour and trusted Jesus Christ to forgive us our sins. We invited Him into our lives and now know we shall meet Mummy some day in heaven.

"Sadly, Daddy died almost four years ago. We miss him greatly and appreciate his courage in the face of the tragic loss in our home.

"I see God's purpose in taking Mummy. It was to introduce us to a Christian house-keeper, who in turn introduced us to Christ."

Everlasting Arms

Everlasting Arms I need You
Everlasting Arms I feel You
Underneath and round about me
- setting mind and spirit free.

Everlasting Arms enfold me
Everlasting Arms please hold me
In the strength of Your embrace
'till I run my earthly race.

Everlasting Arms will help me
Everlasting Arms will keep me
- underneath and round about me
'till I see Christ face to face.

NO BLAME - JUST PAIN

Philip was a healthy fifteen year old, full of the joys of entering his teens when he would explore a new world through his many and varied interests.

He arrived home from school as usual one winter's day. With the hours of sunlight being so short, he looked at the clock and knew he could fit in some training before Mum would serve the evening meal.

The cross-country race would take place in Edinburgh the following weekend, so he decided to do 'a lap', which would take him round a country road near his home, back along the footpath of a main road leading to the local town.

Philip was unaware of the lurking danger and in the glare of blinding traffic lights collided 'head on' with a lad cycling back to base having completed his paper round. Philip's head hit the concrete path.

Philip's mother, Beryl, had had a busy day with her adopted family. As a registered child-minder, her day was full caring for several active pre-school kids. When the doorbell rang, she had no idea what sad and devastating news she was going to hear!

Fortunately, at this stage, Philip was still alive, but she knew she had to act quickly and prepare herself to face the unknown. There was no time to panic, no time to deliberate or make plans for either an evening meal or the future.

Bob, Philip's father, was not home from work when Beryl and her daughter, Michelle, received the news, but arrived shortly afterwards. He and Beryl drove to Craigavon Area Hospital to find Philip unconscious. In those unforgettable moments, they hoped against hope that things would change, praying fervently for his recovery. He was placed on a life support, but Philip never gained full consciousness and went, three days later, to his eternal home.

The days ahead were not easy, but with kind neighbours and friends, the family felt supported.

Letters poured in daily expressing sympathy, love and appreciation of Philip's short, but fulfilled life.

A teacher at Portadown College, where Philip was a promising student, wrote…

"When Philip returned to us in September past, after the summer holidays he had gained not only in height, but also in maturity. In short, I believe that Philip had realised that life has many rich rewards for those who are willing to get involved and not sit passively on the sidelines.

"Philip's passing has been felt deeply by us all. There were few dry eyes in the college last Thursday when the news emerged that Philip wouldn't be coming back to school.

"Next week, next month, next year and for a long, long time we're going to miss the quiet, fair-haired lad who stood with his friends down the corridor during break and lunchtime.

Yet we are grateful for his life and witness to all who knew him. The qualities, which you, as his parents instilled in him from an early age certainly bore fruit – he was a credit to his family.

"Philip got a lot out of life but he also put much into it. Not least he has given us a fine example of a delightful young man and many, many happy memories."

Home

Gone to his dear Saviour
- forever now to be
in His immediate presence
from sin and sorrow free -
we miss the friendly welcome,
the words of hope and cheer,
but memories we will treasure
of one whom we hold dear.

Gone home– we're sad and lonely:
no smile, no words we hear!
No thoughtful card or present
brings us pain - and oft a tear!
But there's a bright tomorrow
on heaven's golden shore -
once more we'll be together,
with Christ forevermore

This poem is
dedicated to the
memory of Philip.

I asked Beryl recently if she ever blamed God for the death of her youngest son. Her reply deeply moved me. She said that neither she nor Bob blamed God for taking their son.

Bob and Beryl have found – In acceptance lies peace!

"As for God, His way is perfect... He is a shield for all who take refuge in Him".

Psalm 18:30

Bob and Beryl Johnston write:

"We cannot tell you it was easy to say "Goodbye" to Philip – It was heartbreaking!

"We left the hospital with heavy hearts and quickly had to make major decisions, arrange a funeral and go forward into the irresistible future. Our son, Brian and daughters, Michelle and Cheryl, were a source of strength to us as together we shared the grief. It was a learning process for us all. We had to give each other space to cope with our individual grief, yet we needed each other, and our wider family and friends, for help and support.

Following our bereavement, we were consumed with weariness. At the same time we were carried along by the Grace of God and by the prayers and support of many friends.

"Our beloved pastor, Rev Desmond Knowles was a tower of strength, and to him, we will be forever grateful.

"We share our experience with you, praying that God will use it to help you cope with your grief and find hope in the fact of a glorious reunion in Heaven."

MOTHER'S LAST WORDS

I have very fond memories of my dear mother, Margaret, who entered the presence of the Lord in 2003. Parting with mother was not easy, as she had been my best friend, and had always been there for me, throughout my childhood, teenage years and even after I got married.

I can remember many of the things she said and did. But the abiding memory of my mother is the last words she said before she left us. As our daughter, Rachel, held her in her arms, mother said, "I'm going home."

During her lifetime mother lived in a number of different homes. There was the home into which she was born on 23 April 1917. Then there was the home she and my father set up when they were married. When mother was widowed she spent a number of years in two other homes. All of these had one thing in common – they were just temporary homes.

The last unforgettable words, "I'm going home" are a precious memory! A few moments later she finally arrived at her permanent home, in Heaven. She was welcomed into her new home by Jesus, who was fulfilling the promise He made when He said, "I go to prepare a place for you… that where I am, there you may be also." John 14: 2; 3

Mother had been looking forward to going home since the day, during her eightieth year, she had put her faith in the Lord Jesus Christ. On that day she realised that Jesus had died on the cross as her substitute and by doing so, had paid in full the penalty for the guilt of her sins.

Every night before mother slept she read a portion of the Bible she kept on her bedside locker. In the Old Testament she read what the prophet Isaiah wrote about the Lord Jesus Christ. He said, 'Surely He [Jesus] has borne OUR grief and carried OUR sorrows; yet we esteemed Him stricken, smitten by God, and afflicted. But He was wounded for OUR transgressions, He was bruised for OUR iniquities; the chastisement of OUR peace was upon Him, and by His stripes we are healed. All we like sheep have gone astray; we have turned every one to his own way; and the Lord has laid on Him the iniquity of us all' (Isaiah Ch.53 vs. 4-6).

Mother invited the Lord into her life and asked Him to be her Saviour. From that moment on she had a wonderful peace in her heart and the assurance that one day she would be welcomed into her Heavenly home by Jesus.

Since my dear mother went home, I have missed her every day. I miss her on her birthdays, at Christmas time, on the anniversaries of her passing, but especially on Mother's Day. While others friends have the joy of presenting bouquets of flowers to their mothers, I visit the cemetery and lay the flowers on my dear mother's grave. The loneliness and the pain of being separated from one who loved you so much are very real.

However, the Lord has continued to sustain me by giving me the assurance that one day mother and I will be reunited again in that place where there shall be 'no more death, nor sorrow, nor crying nor pain' (Revelation Ch.21 v. 4). I know I will meet her again when I arrive home. In the meantime I have great peace in my heart, for I know that mother is safe in the arms of Jesus. Mother is at home!

Mary Keogh

B. Hunter
2008

Will your anchor hold in the storms of life

THE GIFT OF CHILDREN

The Bible teaches us that children are "a heritage" from the Lord - a special gift to parents in a secure relationship.

Pause to thank God for children and pray for their protection in an evil society. Pray for those who have gone through the trauma of losing a child and for those who are not able to have children and would like to have a family.

Heather and her husband were disappointed when it seemed they would not be able to have children. They were happy together and knew that God had a purpose for both of them with or without children. He had clearly brought them together to share their journey through life in the bonds of marriage. What a joy when baby Faith arrived!

The proud parents had the unexpected gift of a sweet child who is full of fun and is enjoyed by all their family and friends. As a mother, Heather, expresses her joy in poetry...

My Miracle Baby

*The overwhelming feeling when you first hold her in
your arms,*
*The feeling of protectiveness as you promise to keep her
from all harm;*
The pride of knowing that she's a gift from God, to you.
The delight at watching crawling become a wobbly walk,
The day she first turns to you and does her best to talk,
The happiness at holding her and hugging her so tight,
The loveliness of kissing her as you say 'goodnight'.
The joy, as you play with her and get to know her ways,
*The memories of the early moments stay with
you all your days.*
*And as the weeks turn into months and
eventually to years*

You look back on all her growing and remember, with laughter and tears.

For that is what it's like to be a mother, at least it is to me,

For my beautiful daughter, Faith, was not supposed to be!

Yet God granted me the privilege to have my precious baby,

And so it is with God - there are no "ifs" or "buts" of "maybes."

There is only His sovereignty, His power and His plan,

So through my little baby, Faith, I pray others will see His Son,

And realise that in their lives, Jesus should be number One.

Heather Rowe

A PILLAR IN THE TEMPLE

My father died in November 1983. It is almost twenty five years ago now, but I still miss him and grieve for him. Many things have happened in those twenty five years that I would love to have told him about, and in so many situations, I have craved his wise counsel.

It was a Saturday morning. My mother and he were getting ready to re-decorate the hall, stairs and landing of our home. My father was going into the roof space to store some items when the bolts which held the "Slingsby" ladder into the roof space gave way and he fell back, hitting his head on the wall and fracturing his skull. He died two days later. It was Remembrance Day weekend.

I remember the Saturday evening in hospital as my mother and I sat with my father in his unconscious state. We sat quietly, praying and hoping that in some miraculous way he would regain consciousness. The TV at the other end of the ward carried the sounds of the Festival of Remembrance from the Royal Albert Hall. On Sunday morning, we were still sitting there, watching my father, as he inhabited that twilight world between life and death. The TV sounds of the bands and the bugles from the Cenotaph at Whitehall were the backdrop to our vigil. At 11.30am on Monday, he passed away.

Six weeks previously, he had retired from his work. For years, my mother had attended my grandmother who was disabled with arthritis, and who then came to live with my parents during her final years. However, she had passed away the previous year and my mother and father were looking forward to the opportunities and the time together that retirement would bring. Now, in an instant, that was all taken away.

I remember some of the visitors to our home. One of our neighbours, a lovely Catholic woman, cried as she stood beside my father's coffin, and then she gently kissed him. It made me cry, and still does, as I remember it. I remember the text that was preached at his funeral. "I will make him a pillar in the temple of my God" from Revelation 3. That summed him up perfectly.

My mother didn't come to the graveside. As an only child, I seemed to stand there alone. A colleague came to shake my hand when the service was over, and quietly whispered:

"The souls of believers are at their death made perfect in holiness and do immediately pass into glory while their bodies, being still united to Christ; do rest in the grave until the resurrection."

I believed those words that day in a way I had never believed them before.

About ten months after his death, my mother sent me into the garage to get something and his boots and waterproof clothes were still hanging there in the garage, and I cried as I remembered him. I still have the New Testaments with his notes attached that he carried with him and used as he spoke at the open-air service in the middle of the town every Saturday afternoon. I remember him today as a man who loved his Saviour, loved his church, and loved people. I still meet people who speak of him with such warmth and of how he helped them. I am comforted when people talk about him and recall his words and his kindnesses. I am just sad that my children didn't get to know their grandfather, but we shall meet again.

One of my predecessors in Kells and Esylane was Rev. James Houston. A member of the congregation told me how he came to see her after she had suffered bereavement. He said,

"Heaven is brought that bit closer to you now."

In the intervening twenty five years, I have lost a lot of friends because of death, but they are "with Christ which is far better". Some days it seems as though heaven is very close.

Stafford Carson.

A FUTURE AND A HOPE

Fifteen years ago, I suffered bereavement through the loss of my husband. This had been a long and happy marriage and we were both involved in caring professions.

Those who have experienced the death of a spouse would know that it is a devastating and shattering experience and something that cannot really be prepared for, and that is how it was with me. The darkness, the emptiness, the loneliness, the sorrow and pain, I had no future anymore. I wasn't a wife, I wasn't the single person, I was before my marriage, I felt totally inadequate; this was how low I felt before the Lord began to heal me.

I learned about healing from a Minus One Group. Minus One is part of EM Focusfest Ministries, and was formed for the support and encouragement of widows (that dreadful name).

At my first support group session I was introduced to others who were on the pathway of healing. It was great to be part of this group who knew exactly how I felt and could really support, encourage and pray for me on a daily basis, and the Lord began to heal, like a burn, skin on skin. He slowly changed my life, introduced me to areas of His work previously unknown to me. This was certainly not a pain free experience, I shed many tears and it took a long time to move through the grieving process. Many good friends helped me, but it did happen. I am healed from my brokenness and have come through the process to emerge as a different person; God's person, a person who has been moulded and reshaped but who still longs to stay in the Potter's hand to be used by Him in whatever way He thinks fit.

Jeremiah 29:11 has been a real strength and encouragement to me:

"For I know the thoughts that I think toward you, says the Lord, thoughts of peace and not of evil, to give you a future and a hope."

I have proved this through these recent years. He has given me a future and I thank God for the experience of bereavement because without it I would never have fully known the goodness of God. I know His love in a way that I never did before. I see it in His care and protection and in His planning – a tailor made plan just for me.

Margaret McCormick

Comfort

God has arms strong enough
to hold the universe,
yet gentle as a mother
He will come and ease the stress
of weary pilgrims on the road
to everlasting bliss!
His arms caress, He gives the kiss
of peace to troubled breast.

MEMORIES TO TREASURE

The memories of Timothy Joshua Agnew will be treasured forever by his devoted parents, the wider family circle and friends, and by the staff who nursed him in the Royal Belfast Hospital for Sick Children and Birmingham Children's Hospital. Everyday of Timothy's short life was special to his Mum and Dad because he was such a happy child and never complained, but with a remarkable acceptance of his quality of life, he endeared himself to all who had the privilege of knowing him. Timothy's mother, Tracey, had a special bond with her son that made the parting more difficult: because she was attending to his physical needs on a daily basis, she was both mother and nurse. No doubt, it was that relationship that enabled Tracey to love her son, while at the same time, not allow pity to rule her emotions: her child needed her and that was the most important part of her daily routine. Father too shared the tasks, as together they devoted themselves to parenting the precious gift God gave to them for six and a half years.

Born on 27th November, 1997, with Chronic Intestinal Pseudo Obstruction Syndrome, Timothy lived as normal a life as possible. He attended school, Boys Brigade and Sunday School and enjoyed activities with the many friends who always wanted to be in his company, and treated him as 'one of the boys'.

He spent a lot of time in The Barbour Ward in the Royal Belfast Hospital for Sick Children, which meant he made friends there too, but wherever he went, he brought cheer and inspired others by his perseverance and determination to face each difficult day. The Barbour ward became his second home – he loved hospital.

During the last three months of his life, he was a patient in the Birmingham Children's Hospital for a bowel and liver transplant, where the staff and the hospital chaplain could not have done more for Timothy and for his parents.

On 28th June, 2004, the long fight for life was over, as Timothy went to be with Christ. His last words will be the lasting memory of his parents…

"You know Mum and Dad loves you?"

"Yes."

"Do you love Mum and Dad ?"

"Yes."

"You know God loves you?"

"Yes."

"Do you love God?"

"Yes."

If you were to ask Tracey and Ronnie if the parting was painful, their answer would be - "Yes." But they have been upheld by the love and prayers and of their many friends. Ronnie's grief was immediate, while Tracey could not grieve, but bottled her sorrow for some two years. She found help with Care in Crisis and was given excellent counselling. It took time for her to be able to say, with Job…

"The Lord gave and the Lord has taken away…"

When she came to the words -

"Blessed is the Name of the Lord", Tracey found that difficult, until one day she heard the hymn sung to the words of Job 1: 21…

"He gives and takes away:
He gives and takes away:
But my heart WOULD CHOOSE to say…
"Blessed be the name of the Lord!""

Timothy has gone to his eternal Home. No more discomfort and pain, no more treatment, and although Mum and Dad will miss attending to his every need, he does not need the physical attention any more – He is with Christ and that means all is well. When Ronnie and Tracey are reunited with Timothy Joshua, he will be changed and have a glorified body.

"We shall not all sleep, but we shall be changed – "in a moment, in the twinkling of an eye, at the last trumpet. For the trumpet will sound, and the dead will be raised incorruptible, and we shall be changed." 1 Corinthians 15:51; 52

God gave to your parents
A bundle of joy:
Bright little fellow –
At times would annoy!
But you were the sunshine
Of McCormick's first home;
Mum and Dad loved you –
Their very own son!
Your crying and laughter
With Martin and Myles
From toddler to teenager
You oft' made us smile!
From childhood to manhood
You took life in your stride:
Your dreams of the future
You cherished inside!
But God had a purpose
Far higher than yours
And took you to Heaven
At just eighteen years!
We don't understand it
But know God was right!
So Mike till tomorrow –
We just say GOODNIGHT!

This poem was written when my 18 year old nephew died as a result of a road accident in Zimbabwe, 5th April, 1986.

(First published in "The Fragrance of Truth" by Vera Smith in 1987)

SAFE IN THE ARMS OF JESUS

In the picturesque village of Richhill, a young couple struggled to accept the death of their precious baby daughter.

Wilfie and Linda had two healthy sons Andrew aged six and Peter four when baby Christine arrived. There was great excitement as father and boys came to greet the new arrival. She was a gift to their already happy family and they were delighted.

"It's a girl!" Congratulations! Family and friends were thrilled it was a girl too – gorgeous little pink baby clothes and toys came in abundance. With two boys, this was the icing on the cake for the whole family. Christine was showered with love and gifts on her arrival!

Sadly, the rejoicing was turned to sadness when it was discovered that their darling daughter was born with an medical problem. At first it was diagnosed as Hirschprung's Disease, but later tests revealed an unusual metabolic disorder that would necessitate a lot of hospitalisation and medication, with no promise of a long-term future. Linda and Wilfie struggled with the prospect, not realising that approximately six months of her short life would be spent in the Royal Belfast Hospital for Sick Children. This proved difficult as father worked full time, shared the burden of their daughter, and cared for two small boys at home. Linda and Wilfie commuted between Belfast and Richhill, weary in body and distressed in mind, as well as learn the techniques of continuing the medical procedures when Christine was at home. It was their faith and trust in God's love and strength that kept them going! Psalm 121 was a great comfort to them as they lifted their eyes to the only source of help in their situation.

Born on 27th July, 1989, Christine was God's gift to a family whom He knew could handle a special task – love and care for a family member who was dependent on their strength. It was not easy! Linda writes:

"Christine died on 2nd May, 1990. When she died I thought my life was over, part of me was missing and my family would never be complete again. But then I realised that she was a perfect little girl, she would suffer no more pain, and nobody could hurt her now that she was safe in the arms of Jesus - but the pain of parting with her was almost unbearable.

My husband was also devastated when our daughter died, but when the pain of missing her was really bad for one of us, the other one remained strong and able to comfort. There have been many times when I have yearned to hold Christine in my arms just one more time, to feel her soft baby skin and smell her delicious baby smell, but only God could love her more. Christine was our gift from Him for only a short time, He wanted her back and we had to let her go. Almost eighteen years later I still miss her so much and the tears still flow as they are now as I write this. Birthdays, anniversaries and Christmas are very difficult times, but I am certain that she is safe where she is and that one day my family will be complete again. We had to keep strong, we had two young sons to care for; they had lost a sister, and many nights we had to dry their tears and try to explain why their sister had gone to heaven."

With the help of family and friends, Wilfie and Linda live busy and fulfilled lives. Their experience of loss has enabled them to help others, as well as become involved with voluntary caring organisations. They have found blessing out of buffeting and despite the pain, they know that, "as for God, His way is perfect!"

MUM IS AT REST IN HEAVEN

When Judith Henderson's mother died, she was devastated. Her relationship with her mother had always been very close, but the mother and daughter bonds deepened as Judith was expecting her second baby. Mother had been there for her first pregnancy so once more Judith sought her wise counsel. Sadly, as her illness progressed she needed all her strength to cope with her weakness and depended more and more on family members.

There were endless questions in Judith's mind, but there was no time to search for answers, as she and the others lovingly cared for her mother. What a wonderful patient and what loving devotion to a mother whose exemplary life deserved the best! Their family had always been closely knit but the bonds tightened as hope came and slowly ebbed away over a number of moths. In April, 2002, the family had to release their hold as a much loved wife and mother left her family and went to be with her Saviour.

Judith was sandwiched between an older sister and a younger brother -they were a happy family with secure foundations, and her parents brought the three children up with special emphasis on their spiritual welfare. However, when Judith started secondary school, she began to want more than, what she called, the "CHURCH THING".

In her own words -

"I just lived for the weekends, going out with my friends and not coming home until the early hours, never thinking what it was doing to my parents and probably not even caring."

A whole new chapter opened in the life of the young wife and mother. Now that her own mother was gone, just two weeks before her little girl was born, she had time to ask the questions but no answers were forthcoming. Why did it happen to me? I needed my mother! Why did it happen to someone who was so good in every way? She felt unable to cope and the only way she could drown her thoughts was to party at least once a month. As long as her husband, whom she loved dearly, was fine, and Aaron and Ellen were provided for, she thought she wasn't doing anything wrong.

Then things started to change. Her closest friend started to attend church and talked about joining the choir. Judith found it difficult to understand but had seen a marked change in her life. She felt she was losing her and wondered if she had done something to cause a breech in their friendship – then her friend told her she had "given her life to the Lord." The change was obvious: she had a sense of calmness and peace within her – something Judith longed for! Fear gripped her heart for she had lost her partying friend and didn't know how she would get through life without her.

Things began to happen that were not part of human planning. A desire to know God personally was welling up within: she found herself going home from work one night to pray for help and guidance, something she had not done for a long time. Her whole thought pattern was changing from personal enjoyment to a personal need for God to release her and give her a purpose for living – then at the end take her to heaven where she would be reunited with her mother.

On Sunday, 29th May, 2005, it happened. Judith describes it –

"I opened my heart to the Lord and I have walked beside Him ever since."

Like Job, she cried out…

"O that I knew where I might find Him!"

Judith found Him when she searched for Him with all her heart! She found Him when she stopped trying and trusted: when she received Him as her Saviour and Lord.

The search has ended for Judith! In Solomon's words of wisdom, she can say…

"I am my beloved's,

"And my beloved is mine."

Song of Solomon 6:3

HELPFUL LITERATURE

Many have found an oasis, when the journey was tough, through reading of others who coped with similar situations. Books can be a real source of encouragement, especially when you are lonely and there is no one to share your burden. Make new friends through books: someone has described reading as "entering another persons mind without the intrusion of their personality." If you are not a reader, don't try to read too much at a time but read slowly and think through the content. You may not agree with everything but at least you are discovering how another person has walked through their valley of bereavement. The beauty of books is that you can pick one up at any time and find something that will help you in a difficult moment.

The Bible has all the answers to life's problems. You will find words of comfort, promises you can claim and words that will help you in your understanding of sorrow and loss. The Psalms are particularly helpful: the New Testament truth and teaching is instructive and comforting: the letters of Paul have much to teach on bereavement and on life after death: the Book of Revelation gives us an insight into what heaven will be like and whets our appetite for our eternal destiny.

There is excellent reading material in bookshops. Talk to the assistants and they will guide you in your selection of books to help your particular need: the many grief related organisations want to help you and will recommend helpful literature, tapes and CD's.

May you find Joy in the Morning a help as you travel the lonely road of bereavement, and await the happy reunion in heaven, when "the day dawns and the shadows flee away."

"To everything there is a season,

A time for every purpose

under heaven:

"A time to be born,

And a time to die;

A time to plant

And a time to pick up what is planted:"

"A time to weep,

And a time to laugh;

A time to mourn,

And a time to dance;

"I know that whatever God does,

It shall be forever.

Nothing can be added to it,

And nothing taken from it."

Ecclesiastes 3:1; 2: 4;14

"Worthy is the Lamb!"